Retirement Investing

A
No Nonsense
No Hype
Guide to:

Retirement Decisions
Protecting Your Assets
Preserving Your Purchasing Power
Making Your Money Last
Having Adequate Income
Passing on the Most to Your Heirs

Michael L. Rosenberg
Registered Financial Consultant

D1044568

Table of Contents

What Can you Get Out of This Book?

In my years as a financial advisor to individuals, I have seen so many expensive investing mistakes. Smart, knowledgeable people make errors in their investments that cost them thousands and hundreds of thousands of dollars in lost principal. I wrote this book to help you avoid these mistakes.

We are in an age of do-it-yourself. An investor can make his own investments and has plenty of help - magazines, on-line services, the Internet, investment newsletters, etc. There is no shortage of knowledge out there, but you may still feel starved for the right information.

These sources mentioned can explain the thousands of investment options available. When you think about it, there are literally millions of different ways you could put together your own portfolio, given the number of options. *But none of these sources can tie it all together for your personal circumstances.*

That's where a financial advisor comes in. I may be biased because I advise people about their investments for a living. But I need to tell you that for the small percentage that people pay me for expert advice, they can save many times this amount just avoiding mistakes.

What people often do not realize is that the **goal** of investing is **NOT to make money**. The **goal** is to <u>**not lose**</u> **money**. And avoiding losses means avoiding mistakes.

My job is helping people avoid those costly mistakes. It's just too hard to make up the loss on a bad investment with your "good" investments.

The most significant mistake that investors make is investing with their emotions. You may think you're calm and collected, but most people aren't. Take this quick test:

1. Have you ever sold a stock and then see it continue to climb a lot more, because you were afraid that if you held on, you'd lose the profits you already had?

2. Have you ever held a losing stock for months or years and never seen it recover?

3. Do you own any investments that you inherited and you keep them for sentimental reasons, even though your money might be better invested elsewhere?

4. Do you have more than 30% of your portfolio in treasury bills and FDIC insured bank accounts because you're afraid of losing money?

5. Have you avoided writing a will or trust because you're superstitious about planning for death?

If you answered yes to any of these questions, you're managing your money with your emotions. This is extremely dangerous. Your emotions will almost always guide you in the wrong direction when it comes to money.

My advice has always been:
Use your *heart* for your *family*.
Use your *head* for your *money*.

Because it's hard to separate your emotions from your money, a financial advisor can be extremely valuable. Your advisor can keep a calm head and advise you to take the proper actions when it's difficult for you to do so because your emotions get in the way.

Investors who realize this can start doing much better with their money almost immediately.

In my opinion, an advisor can help you keep the cool head you need for better financial results.

This book is devoted to my clients who have trusted me and realized the financial fruits of a great working relationship.

Ok. Here's what we'll cover on our journey.

3

I've divided this book into **Four Sections**.

In the first section, *I explain how different investments operate.* Investments are the building blocks of our financial picture, so if we understand the building blocks, we start with a good foundation. Regardless of how much experience you have had, you will learn something new in this section.

Once you understand how the investments work, *I will show you how to put together a portfolio*, in Section II.

Section III *addresses the burning retirement questions*, such as:

- How long will your money last?
- How much do you need to retire?
- What do I do with my company plans and pension when I retire?
- Does it make sense to pay off my mortgage?
- Should I get a smaller place or rent?

Lastly, in Section IV, *I show you how to protect what you have created.* I talk about insurance, estate planning and long term care. It does not matter how much you accumulate if you leave yourself open to risks that can wipe you out overnight.

I needed to make up a new English word in writing this book. I wrote this book for retirees and pre-retirees, generally, those 55 and older. I needed one word to describe this group and the word "seniors" was certainly not descriptive of the whole group.

So please indulge my literary creation. *I call this 55 plus group* "matures."

So let's get started with Section I on investments.

Important Note:

There are illustrations in this book that are hypothetical and do not represent a particular investment. They are included to illustrate a concept only and should not be considered indicative of actual rates or terms available. The market for all securities is subject to fluctuation such that, upon sale, an investor may receive more or less than their original investment.

SECTION I

INVESTMENTS
&
HOW THEY WORK

Money Market Instruments – *The Preference for Liquidity*

Since this book is written for matures, let's first talk about liquidity, something that matures seem to prefer in their investments (although you will soon learn, has a very great price). *Let's discuss these liquid instruments that we call Money Market Instruments.*

These are investments that pay a very low return but are highly liquid:

- **Savings accounts**
- **Checking accounts**
- **Treasury bills**
- **Money market accounts**

Most matures are lulled into the **FALSE SAFETY** of these investments. Let me show you why.

First, let's take a look at **bank accounts**. Bank investments typically pay, let's say, 4%. After we take away taxes and inflation, we have a negative return.

Interest on savings account	4.0%
Federal taxes	-1.1%
State taxes	-0.3%
Consumer inflation	<u>-3.0%</u>
Net return to you	<u>**-0.4%**</u>

You must remember that while your money sits in the savings account for the year, the prices at the supermarket are rising about 3%. This inflation *must always be subtracted from any investment return* so that we see how much we are really ahead. **And in the case of the savings account, we're not ahead, we're behind!**

Economists call this the
Real Return
because it's really what you are receiving.
Look at the difference over **10 years:**

Start with $100,000		
	Balance in Passbook (no Withdrawals)	Real Earnings, after taxes & inflation
Year 1	104,000	99,600
Year 2	108,160	99,201
Year 3	112,486	98,804
Year 4	116,985	98,408
Year 5	121,665	98,105
Year 6	126,531	97,623
Year 7	131,593	97,232
Year 8	136,856	96,843
Year 9	142,331	96,456
Year 10	148,024	96,070

(Assumes tax rate of 31% and inflation rate of 3%.)
Live long enough and you'll be broke!

[1]Investments into certificates of deposits and passbooks are
FDIC insured and offer a fixed rate of return. The market
for securities is subject to price fluctuation

So whether you keep your money in CDs, T-Bills or any of these money market instruments, if you are only getting 4% or 5% and you think that's what you're really earning, you're not doing yourself any favors. You're really earning nothing or even a negative amount.

So why do matures have such a preference for investments with a negative return? **First**, most matures do not realize that they have a negative return. **Secondly**, matures tell me they like having the money liquid in case of an "emergency."

What type of an emergency do you anticipate? Ill health? A nursing home stay? These are legitimate concerns.

The cost of these catastrophes is so great that you could quickly wipe out $50,000 or $100,000 you keep in CDs to cover the cost. While you need to be concerned about these dangerous possibilities, you need to cover these risks as inexpensively as possible.

The cost of "earning" low rates on your money is the most expensive way to cover such calamities. By leaving $100,000 in a bank account for many years to cover these emergencies, you are losing each year to inflation and taxation. Also, if in fact you do need to pay for one of these catastrophes, you may have to say goodbye to that principal because the cost of long term care could easily exceed $150,000 per person.

Here's a much better idea to safeguard your assets:

Instead, get the money out of bank accounts; invest it for a higher return and then use this extra income to get really good insurance for health care and long-term care insurance that can really protect you in case of an emergency. This way, you safeguard your principal as well and I know that is important to you.

Instead of leaving your $100,000 in a 4% CD, try this:

Interest from 20 year corporate bond @8%[2]	$8000
Instead of 4% CD	4000
Amount you are ahead	$4000
Cost to buy full featured long term care policy	2500
You're ahead by each year	$1500

[2]Investments in any security involve fluctuation and may result in a loss of your investment. While CDs are FDIC insured, corporate bonds are not. Additionally, the purchase of corporate bonds may incur commissions and corporate bonds may not be as liquid as CDs. If sold prior to maturity, corporate bonds may return more or less than your original investment. At the time of this writing, corporate bonds rated BB were yielding 8%. Such bonds may not be appropriate for every investor.

You could be ahead by $1500 (so plan a vacation) and you have more security because you have obtained insurance for the emergency that concerned you.

Wouldn't having insurance be better than just feeling secure because you have a few extra dollars in the bank, when you really know that those dollars won't go very far?

As you'll see in Section II, on putting together your own portfolio, you generally never want to keep more than 10% of your total investments in money market instruments because they do pay such a low rate of return and because after taxes and inflation they do have a negative *real return*.

But when you do put the 10% of your assets in these instruments, you want to get the best possible rate you can.

How? The best rates on CDs can be 1.5% more than the rate at your local bank. You can shop for CDs just like you shop for tomatoes. Any good financial advisor should be able to help you find the best rates.

I also advise the same for buying treasury securities. Many matures will make a trip to a federal reserve office or send their funds directly to the federal reserve in order to save a brokerage commission on buying treasury securities. But this really saves less than many think:

1. If you want to participate in the federal reserve auction, your funds (cashiers check) must arrive at the fed by 11 am Monday morning. This means you need to withdraw the money from your bank on Thursday at the latest.

2. Even though the auction takes place Monday, the fed does not start paying you interest until Thursday. So you have lost 7 days interest at 4% on your $25,000. That's $20 plus the $4 you pay your bank for the cashier's check, **plus** your time and bother. Does this seem worth it to save the $40 fee charged by most securities firms to buy you treasury securities?

3. More importantly, if you needed money from your treasury bills really fast, you could not get it from the federal treasury. They cannot sell your Treasury bill for you if you needed to sell it prior to maturity! However, your financial advisor can!

In fact, you could even take a short-term loan against your Treasury bill and not sell it, only if it is on deposit at your securities firm. *Borrowing or selling is not available when you purchase your treasury securities directly from the fed.*

So, if you like the idea of perfect liquidity, getting the best rates and having the most convenience, you will find that your financial advisor is a one stop shop for even your liquid funds.

Besides, wouldn't it be nice to get one statement every month with all of your accounts listed?

By the way, take a look at the following chart. Holding money in the bank or even under your mattress will not eliminate risk. Cash, for example, carries the risk of erosion by inflation. By mixing different types of assets in your portfolio, as we will see in Section II, you might offset the risk of one investment with another.

RISK YOU CAN NEVER ELIMINATE IT

But with a diversified portfolio, you can attempt to offset it

Types of Risk			
	Decline of Original Investment	Inflation	Reduction of Income
Cash	No	Yes	Yes
Bonds	Yes	Yes	No
Stocks	Yes	No	Yes

Investing for Income – *Bonds*

Next, let's take a look at bonds. **Bonds are very simple instruments in concept.** A bond is simply this: *you are lending your money.* You are making a deposit with an institution and that institution is in turn making two promises to you.

The *first promise* is that they will pay you a fixed rate of interest during the term of the bond, and the *second promise* is, at the maturity date, they will return your principal to you. So, it's a very simple investment where you're getting a fixed rate of return and your principal is being returned at maturity.

Who will borrow your money and make these arrangements with you? Well, there are several entities. First, we have the Federal Government. They will sell you treasury securities. In effect, they're borrowing money from you, they're paying you a fixed rate of interest and the second promise is that they will return your principal at the maturity date, which you choose. You choose a one-, five-, or ten-year bond: most any maturity date is available.

Who else will do this with you? Any municipal or state government will do **tax-free bonds** with you. They will borrow your money, pay you interest and guarantee your principal at maturity. Foreign governments, any national government you can think of, in Europe or South America or most other places in the world. You can lend your money to the Government of Malaysia or the Government of Mexico or the Government of Canada, just like you can to the Government of the United States, and they will pay you interest. And they will guarantee your principal at maturity.

Please note, when you do invest in foreign bonds, it's not that they are less safe (the bonds may be just as creditworthy), but please do remember when you invest in foreign securities, your money is subject to fluctuations of the foreign currency (and the entity's solvency). So you may wind up with more or less when your bond matures, not because the bond has gone down or up in value but because the foreign currency has changed relative to the U.S. dollar.

I can't go into details about this here (that's a more advanced topic), but you can certainly inquire if such foreign bonds might make sense for you. These bonds are often very popular because interest rates are often much higher than in the U.S. These bonds have also provided numerous investors with protection of the *purchasing power* of their money as the US dollar has lost value since the mid-1980s.

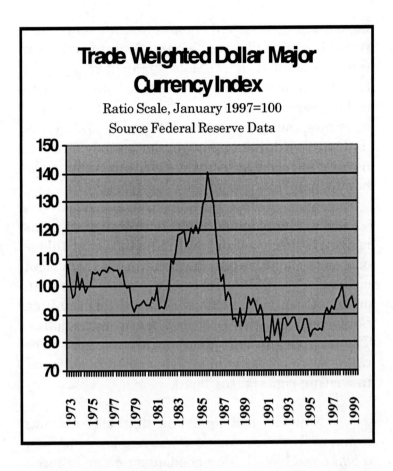

Trade Weighted Dollar Major Currency Index

Ratio Scale, January 1997=100

Source Federal Reserve Data

Other types of entities that offer bonds include corporations: i.e., AT&T, IBM, General Motors. They are happy to borrow money from you and make you the two promises, to return your principal at maturity and pay you interest during the term of the bond.

Now, there's one other feature you need to know about that most bonds have. Most bonds have a call feature. And it simply means this: that if you buy a bond from General Motors and it's a ten-year bond, General Motors may have the right to call the bond ("the call feature") from you in seven years. All that means is, instead of waiting ten years, they can come back to you in seven years and say, we'd like to pay you back early. This is never a surprise, it is always written right on the bond when you first buy it.

So, they can't decide this after the fact. This is always disclosed to you in advance that this is one of the features of the bond. You always get either the face value of the bond when they do that, or sometimes they even give you a little premium. Sometimes they give you 102 cents on the dollar. They'll give you a 2% bonus if they exercise the call feature. This again is all specified in advance, in writing right on the bond.

Now the next question might be on your mind, well, *how do you determine a good bond from a bad bond?* Well, it's a good question and there's a rating system that can help you do this.

Actually, there are a number of rating agencies. The best known agencies are Standard and Poor's and Moody's. *These institutions will give a rating to bonds based on their safety.* And the highest rating is "AAA." That's the rating U.S. government bonds get: most other government bonds get the "AAA" rating as well. Next down would be, "AA." That rating is earned by companies such as AT&T, IBM or General Motors. These are large companies with established markets and significant resources to back up their promises to you. And then a notch down we have companies that are single "A." And then the next grade down is "BBB". Now these four top grades, "AAA, AA, A and BBB", as a group are called *Investment Grade Bonds.*

Investment Grade Above BBB
AAA
AA
A
BBB

Non-Investment Grade Below BBB
BB
B
CCC
CC
C

Most conservative investors will stick with this group called Investment Grade Bonds. Other investors who want higher rates of return will take lower rated bonds that may be rated, "BB" or single "B." That's not to say that these bonds are bad, it's just that they do carry a higher degree of risk. But many well-known companies have bonds selling at these rating levels of "BB" or "B." For example, you as the reader might know such companies as

Safeway, Fruit of the Loom, Chiquita Banana or Playtex. These are all well-known household names, yet these companies do not have the same type of financial standing as AT&T and General Motors. They have a lower rating by Standard and Poor's and by Moody's.

Does that mean that every bond, which is not "AAA," goes bankrupt? Absolutely not! Although the rating is an important first step, many other considerations should be taken into account before deciding which is the best bond for you.

Once a company receives a rating, will it always maintain that rating? Not necessarily. Many excellent companies and municipalities are like you or me. Our financial condition may change from time to time and so can theirs. As a result, you may buy a bond with a certain rating and over the years, the rating may change quite a bit. This is another reason to carefully consider many factors in purchasing your bonds.

Now the last and most important feature we're going to discuss about bonds is the length or term of bonds that you should choose. This is where most matures make a very significant mistake. Generally as people age, they have a preference for shorter and shorter-term investments. This is a very dangerous preference - let me illustrate with the following conversation with a retired investor:

"Why do you want shorter maturity bonds?"
"To make sure that the money is available to me."

"Available for what?"
"Well, if I have an emergency then the money is available."

"Well, what if you had a one-year bond, and you had an emergency six months into the bond, you would still have to break the bond or cash it in early. You might take some type of decline in the market value if you did that."
"Well, that's true but on a one year bond that decline in market value couldn't be very much."

"And that's exactly correct. However, the one-year bond pays you, say, 4%. Not a very good rate of return. Instead if you own a thirty year bond, they might earn 7% or 7¹/₂ or 8%. So, they might earn double the income of the one-year bond."
"Well, I can't invest for that long!"

"Why?"
"Well, I won't live that long!"

"Does that matter? In other words, are you trying to spend all of your money just before you die? I think not."

When most people stop to think this through, they'll realize the following: we all have money that we consider **core capital**. Our core capital is money we intend to never spend. *It is money that we keep working, money that we depend on to generate either interest or dividends, so that we do not want to spend it.*

Therefore, your core capital is designed to outlive you.

And that's a very important concept. You must always be thinking about your money outliving you, not the other way around. You don't want to outlive your money. That makes for a very, very difficult time. *So, your money should actually be invested for a period longer than you believe you will live.* That's the only way it will outlive you. And that's the way you have to have it.

Unless, you think you can time it to die broke or die penniless. But I don't think your timing is that good.

So, the objective you want to have with your core capital is to have it earn as high a rate as possible. By planning on your money outliving you, you can make sure that your money will be working and providing for you until the day you go to a better place. The last thing you want to worry about is money when you retire. The one way to insure you won't have to worry is by putting your money to work for you now.

When looking at bonds, let me encourage you to **invest in longer-term bonds to maximize your interest income.** The objective you want to have with your core capital is to have it safely earn as high a rate as possible.

This is a very important statement I'm about to make.

The best way to protect your assets and never have to use your capital to live on, is to make sure your capital is earning as high an income as possible.

If you're generating the highest possible income, your income will be sufficient to live on and you will never need to use your principal.

Let's take a closer look at this idea. If you have all of your money invested at 4% and the cost of living keeps rising, there will come a time when that 4% just is not enough. But if that money was potentially earning 8% (by investing it in longer maturities), the income would stay in front of higher living costs for a much longer time. By potentially earning a higher rate, you reduce the risk that you will need to dip into your principal.

Take a look at the following chart. It shows what happens to the *real purchasing power* of your money if you live on all of your interest (table assumes 4% inflation):

Start with $100,000^3		
	Earn only 4% and withdraw it each year	Earn 8% & withdraw 4% each year.
Year 1	96,000	99,840
Year 2	92,160	100,006
Year 3	88,473	100,331
Year 4	84,934	100,331
Year 5	81,536	101,463
Year 6	78,275	102,271
Year 7	75,144	103,241
Year 8	72,138	104,374
Year 9	69,252	105,674
Year 10	66,482	107,140
	This is what your $100,000 really buys after 10 years if you have spent your interest	This is what your money buys if you earn 8% and only use half of your interest

---

[3]This illustration is hypothetical and does not represent any particular investment. Bonds that are sold prior to maturity will fluctuate with market conditions.

As the previous chart shows, you cannot spend all of your interest and stay even. Your money loses purchasing power. The only way to stay even is:

1. To attempt to earn a high enough rate (e.g. 8%).

2. Only use half of the income, plowing the other half back in to offset inflation.

So, longer-term bonds should generate a higher degree of income and the higher degree of income will attempt to provide a higher degree of safety in helping you preserve your principal.

This may be a total re-orientation in your thinking. Instead of thinking about six month CD's and one year securities and thinking that three years is long term, I'm asking you to reorient your thinking to twenty, twenty-five and thirty year terms as being the terms that you want because you want to maximize your income.

Now you might say, wait, that will cause a problem. My life expectancy is twelve years and if I buy a thirty year bond all I will be doing is passing on to my heirs a bond that they're stuck with for eighteen years.

Well, that's not really true because a bond is a liquid instrument. Most bonds can always be

26

sold on the open market. When they're sold prior to maturity, they're sold on the open market at a value that's either higher or lower than their face value, just like any stock.

So, it doesn't mean your heirs have to sit with the bond. They can always choose when to sell the bond; they can choose a favorable market time to sell the bond when it's equal to or exceeding its face value or they can just continue to hold it and collect the interest. That's their choice, but in by no means are they stuck because you bought a longer-term bond to maximize your income to protect your assets and live comfortably. You need to do what's best for you first, then your heirs will make a decision later about whether to sell or hold securities that you own.

Next, let me talk a little bit about tax-free bonds. Tax-free bonds are generally useful for investors that are paying 28% or more of their income in Federal taxes. For a married couple, that would be taxable income of $44,000 or more, for a single person taxable income of $26,000 or more. (That's your income **after** your deductions.) Those are the people that should be looking at tax-free bonds.

If your income is less than these amounts, tax-free bonds, quite frankly, don't make any sense. The reason is, you can generally make more by buying a bond that is regularly taxable to you.

After you pay the tax you'll still have more income than tax-free bonds pay because tax-free bonds pay a lower rate of income. So, tax-free bonds are not for everybody.

Be cautious. You want to determine your tax bracket and whether tax-free bonds would benefit you or taxable bonds would be best. Your financial advisor has tables that will indicate your tax bracket. Simply bring in your most recent tax return.

I need also to talk about another type of bond that some investors are not aware of.

These bonds are called Collateralized Mortgage Obligations. Here's the concept:

You deposit some money, you make a loan (just like all bonds you're making a loan along with a group of other investors, you're all lending your money at the same time) to an institution and the institution then turns around and lends the money out to homeowners to buy homes.

A federal agency such as Fannie Mae or Freddie Mac or Ginnie Mae will guarantee your security. You don't need to worry about whether the homeowner pays their mortgage or not. You will get your payment each month whether the homeowner pays or not because the federal agency is guaranteeing your principal and your interest.

Therefore, these securities have a high degree of safety.

These securities have an "implied" AAA rating. Although they do not have formal ratings from the rating agencies, many investment professionals consider these securities to have a quality similar to those with an AAA rating, because of the federal agency guarantee as to payment of principal and interest.

These securities have one significant difference as compared to treasury securities - the term of these securities is not fixed. Let me give you an example:

The average homeowner in the United States moves every seven years. So, you would expect that if you lent money to people to buy homes, you would get paid back in seven years, *on average*. That's generally good thinking.

However, when you lend your money in this fashion, it gets spread out and lent to many, many homeowners. Your money gets diversified. Now, some of those people are going to move in two years, some will move in five, but some are going to be in their house ten, fifteen and twenty years.

Therefore, when you make this type of investment, you will be quoted an *estimated life* of your investment, which may be five, seven, eight years or more. That's an estimated time for when you can expect the money to be returned, but it's an estimate, it can change significantly. Therefore, you could incur costs of reinvesting and could be at the mercy of market swings.

There are a lot of factors that I won't go into here, but just know that if you buy a Fannie Mae security or a Collateralized Mortgage Obligation that's guaranteed by Fannie Mae and it has a five year estimated life, you could see principal back in two years, or one year if some people who borrowed the mortgage money move very quickly.

Other people will live in their homes for years and your money will continue to come in over the entire period. So you need to be prepared for that. However, remember at all times your principal is guaranteed and you are receiving the fixed rate of interest that was promised to you at the beginning of the investment on any principal you still have working. As long as you're investing part of your core capital in these types of securities that you never intend to spend, you could have a potentially attractive return and a relatively high degree of safety. Not a bad place to permanently park some money.

Now let's take a closer look at **bond mutual funds**.

An investor can purchase individual bonds as we have discussed or they can purchase a portfolio of bonds in mutual funds. This is merely a personal choice.

Some investors like owning individual bonds because they want to know exactly what they own, when it comes due, what the rating is, etc.

When you purchase a bond fund, you are really purchasing the bond manager. Since the portfolio changes constantly, you will not know which bonds are in the fund. In fact, the maturity range of the bonds can change quite a bit.

If the fund manager thinks that interest rates are falling, he may position the fund into longer-term bonds (20 years or more). Under the opposite expectation, the manager might shorten the maturities to under 10 years. Therefore, if you want more control and more precision in the bonds you own, individual bonds would suit you better than a fund.

How do you find the bond fund that's right for you? You first need to decide, do you want government bonds, tax-free bonds, corporate bonds (mostly for IRA or pension) or convertible bonds?

Once you decide on the category, a financial advisor can assist you with one of many research services, such as Morningstar or Wiesenberger to help you select the funds with the best profile. Then read the prospectus carefully before investing or sending money.

Preferred Shares – *Another Income Source*

Corporations will raise money by issuing preferred shares. These are very similar to bonds. The big difference is that preferred shares have no maturity date. Once you invest in preferred shares, you own them **until**:

1. You sell them

2. They are called by the corporation

Why do investors purchase preferred shares instead of bonds? Generally, preferred shares pay a higher rate. The preferred shares will generally pay 1% more income than bonds of the same company.

This is because if the company ever had financial problems, the bondholders get paid first, before the preferred shareholders. Since the preferreds are second in line to be paid if the company liquidates, the preferred shareholders take more risk and are paid better. As a practical matter, if you buy high quality preferred shares (these are ranked by S&P just as bonds are ranked), such companies are not likely to go into liquidation.

Generally the preferreds are issued at $25 per share. You can invest in these when they are first issued or anytime by purchasing on the stock exchange.

Always check the call feature. I have seen many investors buy preferred shares that paid a high dividend. What they did not realize is that they bought the shares at $30 and the call feature allowed the company to call the shares the following year at $25. The investor experiences a whopping $5 per share loss because he did not check the call feature.

Preferreds pay dividends every quarter. For investors who want to have their income keep pace with current market conditions, there are adjustable rate preferreds. These do not have a fixed dividend, but rather, have a dividend that is usually based upon treasury bill/bond rates. As the interest rates move up or down in the economy, so will the investor's income. There is usually a minimum and maximum rate that is guaranteed. So if you find a minimum rate that is attractive, you can invest and sit tight when interest rates rise and potentially collect more income.

Annuities – *The Investment for Matures*

Let's talk about another investment that's very popular among matures, which is Tax Deferred Annuities.

Annuities are very similar to CDs at the bank. Here's the difference: A fixed annuity investment is like a deposit but rather than putting it in a bank, your deposit is with a life insurance company and the life insurance company guarantees your deposit.

But here's the one big benefit over a CD. The tax law allows the life insurance company to pay you interest and if you re-invest the interest, you do not pay any taxes on it while it's being reinvested.

At the bank, however, even if you're leaving your interest to reinvest, you're going to pay tax on the interest every year. You pay tax on money that you don't even use. With an annuity, you only pay the tax on the money when you withdraw it.

Now some people ask me, "If I eventually have to pay the tax anyway, why bother putting it off?"

The answer lays in a general rule: always pay money as late as possible. Lend me a million dollars today. I can't pay you back tomorrow, but I can pay you back in 50 years, OK? In the meantime, I can live pretty well off the *interest of your million, can't I?*

When you defer taxes to the IRS, you are doing the same. You are borrowing their money to earn money for yourself. It's double compounding - interest on interest and interest on the tax savings. Over time, the amount you can earn on this borrowed money can be staggering.

Here's an example of money invested at 8%. The chart is a comparison of money invested in a taxable deposit and tax is paid each year from the account and money invested in an annuity where the tax is deferred:

$100,000 Invested	Taxable Account Account at 8%	Tax Deferred Annuity 8%
Year 5	126,417	146,932
Year 10	159,813	215,892
Year 15	202,031	317,216
Year 20	255,402	466,095

With the **deferred fixed annuity**, you **accumulate over $200,000 more** than with the taxable account!

Let's say I started the annuity when I was 55. At 75, I start taking the income to live on. The taxable account will give me an income of $20,432 each year. *The tax-deferred account, which is much larger, will give me an income of $37,287 each year.* Which would you rather have?

It is important to defer taxes and let your balances grow as large as possible. Of course, the deferred annuity has a lot of tax built in that will eventually be paid to IRS at your death. But you won't have much need for the money then anyway! The annuity allows you simply to enjoy life more, and have a higher income today while living off the IRS.

So, fixed annuities are popular for people who have, say, core assets from which they do not need a current income. They are highly safe because the insurance company guarantees it and so your principal is always returned to you and then you're getting a fixed rate of interest. Generally, that interest rate changes once a year.

For example, you may invest instead of having a 5% CD in the bank, you could get a $6\frac{1}{2}$% annuity and after the first year interest rates go up, you may get more. If interest rates go down you can get less, but each year you'll get a competitive rate of interest and you have the option to either take your interest out and pay taxes on it or leave it in and not pay taxes. Even though the interest rate varies each year, this is called a fixed annuity because the principal is fixed in value. You can also obtain fixed annuities, which have a fixed interest rate for their term.

What's become very popular in recent years is a variable annuity, which works similarly, except when you invest your money, rather than it going into an account where your principal is fixed, the money goes into investment options. You select which options you want from an available menu. Since many companies offer variable annuities, you have a wide choice of investment options to select.

Obviously, once you invest in such investment options, your principal will fluctuate up and down. (You are accepting risk, which means that you could lose some or all of your entire principal.) These are called variable annuities because your principal varies year to year as does your potential for return. Variable annuities are preferred by people who want the opportunity to get higher returns (and will accept the risk of losing years in the markets) than they can get by investing in a fixed annuity.

It's not that variable is better than fixed or vice versa, it's just that a more conservative investor who wants to take no risk with their principal will take a fixed annuity and the investor who wants a potentially higher rate of return will take a variable annuity. Prior to purchasing a variable annuity, you should always read the prospectus carefully.

The preceding discussion on annuities has addressed the *accumulation phase.* This is the phase when you are depositing money or the money is building up.

How do you get the money out? It's your choice:

1. You can take the whole balance out at one time. I have never seen anyone do this, as there would be one big whopper of a tax bill on the deferred interest all at once.
2. You can make withdrawals whenever you want.
3. You can *annuitize* the annuity.

Annuitization means that you trade in your balance in the annuity to the insurance company. In turn, they give you a monthly income that continues for a period you choose, such as your lifetime or a fixed number of years (the insurance industry calls this *period certain*). Or a combination of your lifetime and a fixed number of years, whichever is longer.

How you take the money out is very flexible and need not be decided until you are ready to get the cash.

One more **benefit to annuities** that's a **"behind-the-scene"** benefit.

Investing in an annuity can help you reduce the taxes that you normally pay on your Social Security income. As you may know, your Social Security income is not tax-free to you. In fact, up to 85% of it is subject to your full tax rate. However, any income that you're generating in an annuity, that you're leaving in an annuity reinvesting, does not appear in your tax return and does not get included in figuring out whether you pay any tax on your Social Security income.

Now obviously the calculations are different for each person depending on their level of income, but here's the general rule: If your income is between $30,000 and $60,000 a year, there's a high probability that by investing in an annuity you can reduce the income taxes that you're now paying on your Social Security income. So, this is a side advantage that can boost your annuity return another 1% or 2% because of this additional tax savings.

Let's take a look at annuity safety.

When you invest in a variable annuity, your money is invested into investment options that you select. A well diversified investment option (one that contains a variety of stocks and bonds) helps to minimize risk.

In a fixed annuity you might wonder, what does the insurance company do with the money that I invest with them? Very simply, the insurance company invests the money, almost all of it, in bonds. And each insurance company is delighted to give you a flyer, which shows exactly what types of bonds they invest their money in.

Remember before we talked about investment grade bonds versus non-investment grade bonds? The insurer will provide you a list of what percentage of their money is in investment grade bonds so that you can see the safety of their investments.

Also, insurance company quality is rated by a couple of different companies. A.M. BEST is one rating company and generally companies that are in the four top grades, -- A+, A, A- and B+ -- are considered secure (not to say that ones that are not in the four top grades are insecure), but those four top ratings are called the secured category. Insurance companies are also rated by Standard and Poor's and we talked about their ratings before. Generally, any company that's a secure rating by BEST and one of the top three ratings by S & P (AAA, AA, A) carries a high degree of safety.

Stock Investing – *You Still Need Growth Potential*

Let's talk about stocks. As a retiree, you

might think, why do I need stocks? What I want to do is get the most income possible and stocks don't really pay a lot of income.

That's correct. First, let's review some facts.

In 1996 the average stock on the New York Stock Exchange paid about a 2 1/2% dividend. That's not a very good amount of income. So, you would never, ever buy common stocks to generate current income. They just don't pay enough interest, enough dividends to make it worthwhile.

Some people get confused. For example, if you bought a stock twenty years ago, you might calculate your dividends today based on the price you paid for the stock twenty years ago and you calculate that you're making 10%:

Dividend   <u>$2 per share</u> = 10% *false* return
Price paid in 1970 $20 per share

But that's not the right way to think about it. You always have to calculate your dividends, what return you're actually getting, based on <u>today's</u> price of the stock:

Dividend   <u>$2 per share</u> = 2% return
Price today $100 per share

If you had put $4 into a bank account 50 years ago, and that had now grown to $100, would you say that your $4 a year interest was a 100% return? No, you would say that you were getting a 4% return ($4/$100). You would look at the interest as compared to the *current value* of the account.

If you own big companies like General Motors, AT&T or Dupont, you have historically made about a 2% or 3% dividend, not more, based on the current value of your shares. Again, stocks are *not* for current income.

Why would you buy stocks? For potential growth. Stocks can grow in value over time and they've done that very well. It doesn't mean they go up in value every year, but if you take almost every ten year period (for example, 1926 to 1935, 1927 to 1936, 1928 to 1937 and so on), you find that in 63 of those 10 year periods you made money and only 2 times would you have lost money.[1] These results are historical and cannot be guaranteed. The market for all securities is subject to fluctuation such that, upon sale, an investor may receive more or less than their original investment.

---

[1] Data from Ibbotson Associates 2000 Yearbook

ONLY **ONE** INGREDIENT
IS REQUIRED FOR
SUCCESSFUL
STOCK INVESTING:
TIME

Chance of making money in stocks:

Any 1 year	72%
Any 3 years	84%
Any 5 years	90%
Any 10 years	97%
Any 15 years	100%

---

[4] This presentation is based on historical information from January 1, 1926 through December 31, 1999 as reported in the Ibbotson Associates 2000 Yearbook. It is not a guarantee of future results.

What's the conclusion from the previous chart? If you invest in the stock market, you must look at it as a 10-year commitment. You cannot judge your results by looking at how the last year went. This does not imply you must keep the same stock for 10 years, but you must be committed to owning stocks for 10 years to potentially give yourself the benefit of history.

Now, why do you need growth? Here's why. If you retire at sixty-five, you may easily live another twenty or thirty years. It's not uncommon and it's becoming more common every day as new medical finds are helping people to extend their life expectancy. You need to be prepared for another twenty to thirty years of living and that's why you have to have some assets that grow in value because your cost of living will surely go up. You need investments that will keep pace with your increasing cost of living.

Life Expectancies

This chart shows ones remaining expected lifetime.

Note: This is an average, with many living shorter or longer. **Recommendation**: be optimistic, plan your money for a long life.

Age	Males	Female
50	26 years	31 years
55	22	27
60	18	23
65	15	19
70	12	15
75	9	12
80	7	9
85	5	6
90	4	5

So, the first question, how much stock should you own? Here's a general rule. The percentage of your investment portfolio that many investment advisors recommend for stock investments should equal 100 minus your age. So if you're 70, 100 minus 70 is 30. 30% of your investment should be invested in stocks.

The next question you might ask is, which stock? Of course, this is a question that everybody wants to know. They want stocks that are going to go up. Now, here's my view about this:

You can't just invest in stocks without having a system. You must use some type of methodology to buy and sell stocks. Now that can be anything from using a money manager, who has a strict philosophy and a discipline on what to buy, when to buy it, and when to sell it. Or you could use a system like Value Line where you buy just the number one rated stocks and then sell them when they get to number two. You can use the Dow Dividend Strategy system or you can use the O'Neil CANSLIM system.

There are a number of different disciplines, but the point is you need to be on some type of system on which stocks to own, when to buy them and when to sell them. While there is no assurance as to how the stocks will perform, you can approach investing in a more logical manner. Otherwise it's very, very difficult and your emotions will get the best of you. You'll be selling when you're nervous and that's usually the wrong time; you'll be buying when everybody else is excited and that's usually the wrong time. To increase your odds of succeeding in the stock market, you need some type of pre-planned system.

Mutual Funds – *Investment of Choice in the 90s*

Now this would be a good time to talk about mutual funds. The *average person* is probably better off buying a growth mutual fund than investing in individual stocks. And the reason is because the mutual fund is professionally managed by a team of experts who are following the stocks, day in and day out. There is no work for you to do. With the help of your financial advisor and after you have carefully read the prospectus, all you need to do is pick the fund or funds to invest in from the beginning.

That choice amounts to understanding what your objectives are. Now there are three basic types of mutual funds. There are growth funds, which invest their money in stocks. There are income funds, which invest their money in bonds and preferred stocks (which are like bonds and seek to generate income). Income funds are obviously for people who'd like to get a monthly check. And then there are balanced funds, which have some stocks and some bonds in their portfolios.

So, for somebody that's trying to develop a mixed portfolio, often these are called balanced funds because they have a balance between stocks and bonds and they don't focus really on either. They do generate some income for somebody who wants some income. More appropriately, balanced funds are for the investor that really wants stocks but by adding the bonds to the portfolio, they get broader diversification and they attempt to reduce the volatility (the up and down fluctuation of the fund).

Before selecting mutual funds, you need to think about the three categories and what you really need. Do you need growth? Is that what you're investing for? If you're investing for growth, you pick some type of growth fund. Growth funds will differ in how aggressive they are. For example, the growth fund that invests in conservative stocks would invest in blue chip stocks like General Motors, Dupont, AT&T, Boeing, and McDonald's.

On the other hand, an aggressive growth stock, a stock fund that is taking more risk, might invest in high technology companies or biotechnology companies. Generally, retired investors would not be suitable for putting large amounts of money in these types of funds. They may be putting small amounts in, in order to have something that might grow for the future, something that they can leave to their heirs, but these funds have a lot of volatility that can do very well in some years and very poorly in others. To have a 30% to 40% return up or down is not uncommon for these types of funds. So you want to first decide if you are investing for growth.

And then once you know that, do you want

a fund that seeks conservative growth or more aggressive growth?

Selecting Funds

The above discussion focuses on selecting the appropriate categories of funds for your circumstances and risk tolerance. This is a far more important decision than selecting the "best" funds. Most investors are too hung up on trying to find the best fund and ignore the more important macro issues of fund category and risk tolerance. This is akin to selecting a nice tie before buying the suit it will accompany.

Specifically, many investors focus on the fund with the best historical track record. This is not the best way to select funds because this method ignores volatility. If you put your money in a fund that is highly volatile (even though it has a great long term track record) will you be able to sleep at night if it's down 20% for the year?

Take a look at the comparison of these 2 funds:

COMPARING TWO MUTUAL FUNDS		
	Fund A	Fund B
10 Year Average annual return	15%	15%
Annual Return 1979-1984	6%	12%
Annual Return 1985-1989	24%	18%
VOLATILITY	± 20%	± 6%

Note that both funds had a 15% annual return over the 10 years measured. But in the slow years 1979-1984, fund B does better yet does not do as well in the fast years of 1985- 1989. But for the 10 years as a whole, Fund B has much lower volatility from year to year. Even though both funds have historically had the same return over time, Fund B is the clear winner with the highest *risk adjusted* return. A good financial advisor has research services that measure such aspects and can help your selection of the appropriate funds.

Let's turn our attention to income funds. What you're looking for is an income fund and that's going to be a fund that invests in bonds. But here again, you can find the fund that invests in government bonds (that would be for the most conservative investor), or tax-free bonds (for somebody who needs tax-free income). You can invest in funds that invest in corporate bonds, which are taxable bonds (which would be good for somebody either in a low tax bracket) or if you're investing money that's already in a pension or in an IRA (because you're already tax-sheltered in an IRA).

So then, if you think, well, I'd like potential for some income, but I'd also like some growth potential, maybe that's what you use a balanced fund for or you use a combination of pure growth fund and pure income funds to reach your objectives. That's the type of thing a financial professional can help you decide. And most financial advisors have track records and they know the funds well, how they've done, how they stand in relation to all other funds and they can help you select funds that are right for you in working toward meeting your objectives. Remember, always read the fund's prospectus prior to investing.

Section II

Designing
Your
Portfolio

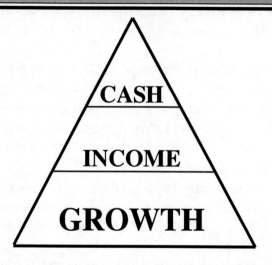

Now you have a good foundation about how
different investments work. We can start talking
about putting together your own portfolio.

You'll notice here a picture of a triangle
divided into three parts.

One part is called cash assets, next is income
and the next is growth. Here's what we're going to
do. First, you need to figure in your own mind,

how much money do you need to live on a month, because first we're going to focus on your income. We are starting first with the middle section of the triangle.

So, let's take an example. Let's say you need $4,000 a month to live on and you get $2,000 from Social Security plus your pension. That means your investments have to generate the other $2,000. So, if we assume that we can get an 8%[5] return on your income investments (on your bonds that we've been talking about previously), that tells us that we need $2,000 a month or $24,000 a year interest from bonds; and if we're getting 8% yield on those, it calculates that we need to allocate $300,000 to income investments in order to produce $24,000 a year in income.

But you say, "Now wait a minute, I don't have $300,000 to allocate to bonds." Well, right off we know there's no possible way to generate the $4,000 a month of income that you'd like using just the income. We will need to use part of your principal each month and to supplement part of the principal, we'll make it up in income so that you can live at the standard of income that you'd like. Now, of course, we try not to use principal in life but for some people it is permissible, as long as the principal will last beyond their lifetime.

---

[5]A hypothetical rate of return and not an indication of a particular investment's rate of return.

We do not recommend that our clients use principal until we have used our software to calculate that the client has enough money to do so. Our computer program can calculate how long your principal will last.

The other case is where you do have $300,000 of assets to allocate toward income and then it's just a matter of building a diversified bond portfolio or using bond mutual funds to allocate that amount so that you're getting sufficient income.

After building your income portfolio, the rest is simple. We put 10% of your investable assets into the cash (or money market) section and the remainder gets invested for growth. Here's an example of an investor with a $500,000 portfolio:

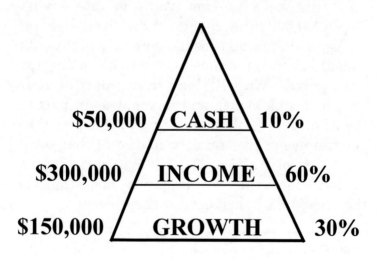

$50,000   CASH   10%

$300,000   INCOME   60%

$150,000   GROWTH   30%

Now any of your assets that you do not need for current income or your 10% liquid cushion could go into growth assets, primarily stocks or growth mutual funds. Now if you're 70 years old, 100 minus 70 is 30% and that would be the portion allocated to growth. 30% percent would be invested in either individual stocks, using some proven system, or growth mutual funds.

Section III
Retirement Decisions

There are a number of questions that come up as we approach retirement. I will answer a number of the more common questions here.

How Much Do I Need to Retire?

Obviously, each person leads a different lifestyle and has a different definition for what is "comfortable." Therefore, on page 58, I have included a chart, which shows how much capital you need to generate a predetermined income.

Let's see how you use the chart. Assume you're 60 and you want an income of $6000 each month. You have $3000 coming from your pension, so you need $3000 from your investments.

On the chart, read across for 60 years old and the column for $3000. This is the amount of principal ($474, 242) you must have **growing at a hypothetical 8%**, in order to receive an inflation-adjusted $3000 a month.

By inflation-adjusted, I mean that you will receive $3120 per month in year 2, then $3244 a month in year 3 and so on. The income you receive will need to keep increasing in order to have the same purchasing power as $3000 today. The chart already factors this inflation effect into the numbers.

Amount of Capital Required to
Provide a Monthly Inflation Adjusted Income

Age	Male Life Expectancy	Female Life Expectancy	Monthly Income Required			
			$2,000	$3,000	$4,000	$5,000	$8,000
Age 55	22.2	27	357,959	536,939	715,918	894,898	1,431,837
Age 60	18.4	22.8	316,161	474,242	632,322	790,403	1,264,644
Age 65	14.9	18.9	271,877	407,815	543,753	679,691	1,087,506
Age 70	11.9	15.3	228,882	343,323	457,764	572,204	915,527
Age 75	9.2	12	185,716	278,574	371,432	464,290	742,864

The figures required are based on male life expectancies. Single women require about 20% greater balances because of their longer life expectancy. The figures indicated assume that the capital is spent completely over the life expectancy. Assumed rate of return is 8% and inflation is 4%. Example: a man age 65 desiring $3000 a month from his investments needs a portfolio of $407,815. The 8% return and 4% inflation figures are hypothetical and do not reflect an investment in any particular security. The market for all securities is subject to fluctuation.

When Can I Retire?

The answer is also provided by the chart on page 59. Simply find the income you want and determine how much principal you need. If you need $300,000 and you have $260,000 already, then you will need to work as long as it takes to sock away or gain another $40,000 of net worth.

When I Retire, What Do I Do with My 401(k), Profit Sharing and Pension from Work?

You often have 2 choices with such plans:

1. Withdraw the funds in a one-time payment.

2. Receive payments over a specified time period (e.g. lifetime).

In almost all cases, I advise you to take control of the money. You can always buy yourself a lifetime annuity if you want and have the monthly lifetime income anyway. By having the money in your control, however, you have more choices.

What if you decide to sell the house in 2 years, use that money and another $50,000 from your retirement to buy a yacht and sail the world? If the money is in your control, you do whatever you please!

Profit sharing and 401(k) accounts can be

rolled over into your own IRA. You simply set up an IRA account with your financial advisor. You give the account number to the payroll people at your company. When you retire, they will transfer your balance to your IRA account. You can then invest the money however you see fit -- into stocks, bonds, mutual funds -- or whatever you and your advisor decide.

As long as you are past age 59½, you can make withdrawals from the IRA at any time (and pay the taxes you owe the IRS). Naturally, it's better to use money that has already been taxed and let your IRA money grow tax, deferred, as long as possible.

Your pension account may not be available to you in a single sum. You may be forced to make a choice among some payment options, such as:

1. A monthly income over your lifetime.
2. A largely reduced income over your lifetime and your spouses lifetime. Your spouse continues to get the monthly amount if you die first.
3. A somewhat reduced income over your lifetime and your spouse's lifetime. Your spouse gets only half of your monthly amount if you die first.

I could bore you with lots of numbers here but I won't. The major issue that people fall prey to is emotional pressure. They take the option that continues the monthly income for their spouse's lifetime also. After all, how can you cut your spouse off?

THIS CAN BE THE WORST MOST EXPENSIVE FINANCIAL DECISION YOU WILL EVER MAKE.

When you select this alternative, you are getting a reduced amount per month. This reduction lasts your entire lifetime. You take this reduction so that your spouse will have the income too. But what if your spouse dies tomorrow? What if you get divorced? These are real life issues that need to be considered.

If your spouse were to die tomorrow, you have given up some monthly income, that you could have had for the rest of your life. Before making such a decision, see your financial advisor for assistance with this choice.

One option that often works well is the following:

1. Take the option that only gives you the highest income with payments over your lifetime.
2. Determine how much life insurance you would need, so that if you died, your spouse would receive the same monthly amount from the insurance company.

3. Find out the premium and use some of your
   larger retirement income to pay the life
   insurance premium.

   Now, if your spouse does die before you, you
can:

A. Close out the policy and take the cash value.
B. Change the beneficiary to your heirs and keep
   the policy.
C. Stop paying and take a smaller paid-up policy.

   Under this scenario, you have lots of choices
and you have not given up any income from your
monthly pension.

What's the Best Way to Invest My IRA/Rollover Money?

   I have met many people who treat IRA
money differently than their other funds. There
is a tendency for investors to be more conservative
with these funds, possibly owning treasury
securities or fixed income investments in their IRA.
Actually, this thinking can have a large cost. This
money is just as important as your other money.
It is part of your overall portfolio and I recommend
that you look at your portfolio as a whole.

   The one difference about your IRA money
is that it is tax sheltered. Therefore, you want to

take advantage of that feature by placing the highest taxed items in your IRA. At the time of this writing, long term capital gains outside of an IRA are taxed at 20%, but if earned and withdrawn from an IRA, could be taxed as high as 39.6% (regular federal ordinary income rates). Therefore, for most people, it makes sense to keep assets that generate long term capital gains (such as stocks) outside of your IRA and put items that generate short term gains (many mutual funds) and ordinary income (fixed income investments) inside your IRA.

Follow the procedure as recommended in Section II on putting together your portfolio. And when you make investments, just place the appropriate investments in your IRA that give you the best tax advantage.

Should I Pay Off My Mortgage?

Generally, the answer is no. If your mortgage is at 8% and you seek to make 10% by investing your money, aren't you ahead by investing the money? Therefore, if you can make more by investing than the rate you are paying on your mortgage, invest the money.

This has generally been true over the last several years. Mortgage rates have been low and investment returns have been high. There is another reason not to pay off your mortgage. If you need money from your house in the future, many banks do not like to lend to retirees. They get nervous when borrowers don't have a job.

So in most cases, it's wise to leave the mortgage alone, or refinance it to get a lower rate.

Should I Sell My House and Rent?

If you want extra income, this can be a very wise move.

Assuming your house has good equity, you can sell the home and use the equity to invest for income, giving you more spendable dollars every month.

RETIREMENT PLANNING	
SELL YOUR HOUSE AND RENT	
Sales price of house	$250,000
Pay realtor	-15,000
You receive and invest	235,000
Investment	235,000
Interest rate	8%[6]
Annual Income	18,800
Less Tax	-4,300
Less Apartment Rent	-9,600
Extra income to spend	**$ 4,900**

[6]A hypothetical rate of return and not an indication of a particular investment's rate of return.

What's the Best Way to Make IRA Distributions?

Generally, investors want the money in their IRAs to grow as long as possible to defer the taxes as long as possible. The IRS requires that you withdraw funds from your IRA starting at age 70$^1/_2$. You can certainly withdraw as much as you want (and pay the taxes), yet the IRS requires a minimum distribution based on your life expectancy. The simple formula is:

$$\frac{\text{IRA Balance} \quad \$100,000}{\text{Life Expectancy} \quad 16 \text{ years}} = \$6,250 \text{ minimum withdrawal}$$

However, the IRS allows you to withdraw the money over the life expectancy of you **and** a beneficiary.

To guard against IRA investors selecting their 5 year old grandson as their IRA beneficiary (and thereby substantially reducing the required withdrawal), a beneficiary more than 10 years younger than the IRA owner is treated as only 10 years younger for purposes of calculating joint life expectancy. The easiest formula is then to subtract 1 (from the denominator above) each year to determine each successive year's required minimum distribution.

If you have several IRA accounts, you must calculate the distribution on the total of all accounts, but you can choose which accounts to make the distribution from. The author highly recommends that you consolidate your IRAs into one self-directed IRA. This will give you as much flexibility as you need for investments, yet simplifies record keeping and distributions.

What's the Best Way to Help My Grandchildren With College?

As we saw before when we looked at stocks, they have historically done very well *over time*. So, if your grandchild has 10 years before starting college, a good growth mutual fund might be a good choice.

If the time period is shorter, you may want a more conservative fund because you cannot afford to be down when the money must be withdrawn for tuition payments. In the past several years, a number of funds have been introduced with a combination of zero-coupon treasury securities and stocks. The growth in the treasury securities insures that your original principal is returned at the end of a specified period. In addition, you will have the value of the growth stocks.

A zero-coupon bond is simply a bond that reinvests its interest rather than making semi-annual payments. A more powerful idea is to invest in a variable life insurance policy. In effect, you select an investment option inside a life insurance policy. If you pass away, your grandchild collects life insurance, which could be worth 3, 5 or even 10 times your investment. The money in the policy grows all tax deferred.

When it comes time for college, if the policy was structured correctly in the beginning, you can simply make tax-free loans (at no cost) from the policy and give the money to your grandchild. If you hold the policy indefinitely, all of the funds will eventually pass to your grandchild, tax-free.

So you can get a nice combination of tax deferred or tax-free growth, a selection of investment options and life insurance on top that can potentially be a big boost to your grandchild's educational possibilities. (Note, loans and withdrawals from a variable life policy will decrease the policy cash value and death benefit. Additionally, depending on performance, you may get more or less than the original amount invested in the policy. There may be penalties or fees associated with loans and withdrawals so the policy and prospectus should be reviewed carefully.)

Section IV
Asset Protection

One of the most critical aspects of mature financial planning and investing is protecting the assets you have already accumulated. Unlike a 35-year-old who goes broke and has plenty of opportunity, there's no earning it back again for a retiree. So, let's talk about that.

First, let me share a story that I heard. In 1991, there was a major fire that burned down 2,500 homes in Berkeley and Oakland, California. Many people in the area lost their homes and many others were not prepared.

I remember one gentleman, who had bought his house in 1971, had insured it for $150,000 and never bothered to look at the insurance again. In 1991, twenty years later, his house was worth $450,000, but he still had $150,000 worth of insurance and that's all he could collect when his house burned down. Unfortunately, this was just plain foolish.

This was just a case of closing one's eyes and hoping for the best, rather than paying attention to protecting your assets. So, let me give you some exercises. You must make some notes and take care of these things this week.

Number one, you need to call the company that has your homeowner's insurance and make an appointment with the agent. Have the agent sit down with you and make sure that:

A. Your home is insured for current value. That you have what's called replacement cost insurance, so that if anything happened to your home, the insurance company would pay to replace it regardless of the value.

B. Have your agent look at your auto insurance policy. Do you have enough liability coverage? God forbid you're out in your car, you hurt somebody, they sue you for $2,000,000. Do you have large enough coverage so that they wouldn't be able to attach your own personal assets, but you'd have enough coverage from your insurance to pay for that type of potential liability?

C. You've got to take a look again at your health insurance. Now if you're retired and over sixty-five, you're eligible for social security and of course, covered by Medicare. Make sure that you also obtain a Medicare supplement policy, often referred to as Medi-Gap. In the Appendix, what I've done is shown you the ten levels of

Medi-Gap insurance that you can buy. Make sure you've got the level that has the coverage that you think you need and think you want or think you have. So, what level you pick is up to you, but let me give you an example.

You may think that if you travel outside of the country and get sick, Medicare or your insurance will cover you. Well, Medi-Care does not and many Medi-Gap policies do not. So, if you're traveling more than a couple of weeks a year out of the country and you want that coverage, you need a better Medi-Gap policy. From my appendix you can see which level of Medi-Gap policy you need and then get that requisite coverage.

The other risk, which you need to plan for, is long term care (nursing home). Medicare and your health insurance DO NOT pay for long term care. Currently, 43% of everyone reaching age 65 spends some time in a nursing home. Do not think you are exempt. The odds are too great that you will need nursing care at home or in a facility at some point in your life.

At $4000 a month, this could wipe you out pretty fast. So if $4000 a month is not readily available to you, please find out about the options for insurance.

Please do not go without this protection. You would never think of driving your car without insurance or leaving your house uninsured. Your health is even more important. After you do the reviews with your insurance agent, and get long term care protection, you have very nicely protected the nest egg you've created.

Risks in Your Life	Chance of Occurrence	Are Your Insured?
House Burning	1 in 88	Yes
Car Accident	1 in 70	Yes
Medical Problem	Yearly?	Yes
Long Term Care	4 in 10	No!

Additionally, if you own a business or have some interest that could bring you personal liability, you must protect it. I saw a gentleman build up a very nice ice cream distribution business. He retired, handed it over to his son and lived off an income that the business generated.

Well his son got into problems, the business was sued and they lost everything. These things happen, but not to those who are protected.

If you have such interests, talk to an asset protection attorney about setting up a family limited partnership or some other device that will protect and segregate any business interests.

This whole arena of asset protection would

be incomplete if I didn't include a small section devoted to estate planning. Many people not only want to protect their assets for themselves, but also for their heirs. If you do not plan ahead, it's easy to watch estate taxes and poor planning rip away the value of your estate.

Estate Planning

First, let me mention the biggest mistake I see most retirees make regarding estate planning. Many, many times, I see a single retired individual who makes an investment. Then they put the name of their son or daughter on it as a joint tenant because they know that when they pass away, their son or daughter will then inherit that asset automatically. This is true. However, such superfluous estate planning can lead to a very severe problem. If that son, for example, happens to be a physician and gets sued for malpractice and the son's assets get attached, legally, the son appears to own half of your investment because your son's name is on it.

Well, your son's creditors could attach that money, which is yours. So, you may not want to expose your assets that way and I strongly advise that you don't. Instead, you probably want to own the investment in just your name, passing it by will, or get a living trust put together so that the name of your trust is on the assets at all times.

This way you don't have exposure to the creditors of your sons or daughters and this keeps everything well protected and, with living trusts you also avoid probate for very quick and immediate transfer to your heirs.

A little more about estate planning. There are some basics that you need to understand. Every individual is allowed to pass $675,000 of assets on to their beneficiaries. Now, there's another great mistake that a lot of married retirees make.

Here's the mistake: The husband has a will and he leaves everything to his wife. The wife has a will and she leaves everything to her husband. Here's the problem that maybe you've never been told before. Each of us has $675,000 (increasing to $1 million in 2006) exclusion on passing along assets to our heirs OR we can leave our exclusion to our spouse. Now, the most important word in that sentence was, "or" because if you go and leave your assets to your spouse, you've lost your exclusion.

Generally, when an attorney draws up a living trust or will for you, what happens is that they segregate the exclusion amount of assets directly to your heirs, not to your spouse, so that you, in fact, get the full benefit of your exclusion. This way, if you're married, you get the exclusion, say $650,000, your spouse gets $675,000 and a married couple can pass a 1.35 million-dollar estate (increasing to $2 million in 2006) to their heirs with no estate taxes. That's exactly what you want to do. For people whose estates are larger, you definitely want to consider the idea of using some type of insurance to pay your estate taxes.

Let me give you an example. Let's say you and your spouse have an estate of one million dollars. Now, that may not be the current value of your estate but you've got to remember, if you're sixty-five years old now, it's very likely that one or both of you might live to age eighty-five or even longer. So, the question is, not what is your estate worth today, but what will it be worth in twenty years.

Your estate, if it's worth a million dollars today, could easily be worth three million in twenty years.

Let's say you have a three million-dollar estate upon death. If that's the case, the first $1.35 million is not going to be subject to estate tax, but the other $1.65 million will and unfortunately the estate taxes are very high. On $1.65 million, you'd pay about $849,700, about 50%, of that $1.65 million for estate taxes.

Total Estate	$3 million
Potential exemption from tax	$1.35 million
Taxable	$1.65 million
Tax	$849,700

Who pays that? Actually your heirs do. It comes right out of their inheritance. So, how do you protect it? It may be very useful to invest in an insurance policy on you and your spouse in the amount of $849,700. What specifically would you do?

The first step is for you get a quote on what it would cost you to buy an insurance policy for $849,700. Now let's just assume that would cost you $20,000 a year. You would have to deposit that in premiums each year, for say 9 years (some policies may become paid up after a certain period of time and no more deposits are necessary).

Now before you shudder that's ridiculous, remember we're going to be saving $849,700. So let's just see if we can, in fact, pay your estate taxes for a heck of a lot less than $849,700.

Let's say you can go out and get an insurance policy on you and your spouse. The annual premium is $20,000 a year. What you do is you take $20,000 a year and you gift it to your children. This helps you reduce the size of your estate and in itself reduces your estate taxes.

Your children then pay the premium on the insurance policy on the lives of you and your spouse. So your children actually own the insurance policy. This is actually very critical that your children or someone other than you and your spouse own the insurance polices. (In fact, if you have life insurance policies right now that you own, please see your attorney, financial advisor or insurance agent right away about why these must be owned outside of your estate.)

Then, when both you and your wife have passed away and the IRS comes knocking for $849,700 in estate taxes, the children merely take the $849,700 they've received from the life insurance company, turn around and pay the IRS and the entire $3,000,000 estate passes to them unencumbered by estate taxes or hopefully, any other liens or taxes. What were the deposits to the insurance company? Probably around $180,000.

So that's the way to pass the maximum size estate to your heirs and certainly look into using insurance because most wealthy people do.

Instead of paying $849,700 out of pocket, you have paid only $180,000 for insurance premiums. A $670,000 savings is hard to beat!

Summary

Doing well financially requires you to understand the ideas in this book and get good professional advice. Advice that has been crafted by experience.

Wall Street loves to create all kinds of confusing investments alternatives - LEAPS, TIGRS, CATS, MIPS, QUIPS, TOPS and on and on. All of these fancy items are some type of stock or bond (or are based on the movement of an underlying stock or bond). If you understand the workings of stocks and bonds as we have explained them, you know most of the basics you need.

Two parting words of advice.

Ignore much of what you read in the financial press. Most of it is hype. One radio talk show host was talking to a group of business people at a private luncheon. He commented on his daily radio announcements and the phrases he used, "The Dow got battered," "GM soared," "Technology issues got creamed." He told the group that he always told investors to take a long term view, but if he went on the radio and advised this every day, no one would listen to this boring advice. He had to make each day sound exciting, like a sporting event!

Secondly, make a plan and stick to it and

ignore the news. There will always be wars, gas shortages, hostage situations, bombings and every disaster imaginable. Your investing should always ignore these passing occurrences. I remember the invasion of Kuwait like it was yesterday. The stock market plummeted, people were scared of the outcome, possible disruptions in oil flow and a resulting recession. I advised investors to ignore this and invest based on their needs, not the front-page news items.

I recall an investor who took my advice. He invested $400,000 into a stock account. When Mr. Saddam had been handily beaten by the U.S., his account proceeded to grow to $600,000 within six months. The client thought I was a stock picking genius. Not at all; there are simple rules of the markets, that when followed, sometimes result in attractive outcomes.

I will not wish you luck because investing well has nothing to do with luck. I do wish you good choices based on sound principals. If we can help you with your financial decisions, we welcome the opportunity to serve you.

Questions?

We would be delighted to answer your questions that we may not have covered in the book. If you need help with retirement planning, we will try and assist you.

You can call me or you can write down your questions and fax them or mail them to me. I may have some brochures or booklets I would be glad to send on the topics that concern you:

Michael Rosenberg, RFC
Diversified Capital Advisors, Inc.
26 Linden Avenue, Suite 205
Springfield, NJ 07081

Phone: (973) 564-6565
       (800) 664-3630

Fax: (973) 564-6564

Note: Parts of this text were written with the collaboration of Larry Klein, MBA, RIA, CPA,

About Diversified Capital Advisors

While, most financial services firms attempt to be everything to everyone (and wind up not specializing very well for anyone), Diversified Capital Advisors focuses exclusively on the needs of those 55 and over and their specific financial problems and opportunities.

Diversified Capital Advisors is a professional firm working exclusively with mature senior investors to protect their financial assets and standard of living. Services provided:

- **Estate Planning** - We show how to avoid estate taxes which are paid by single people with estates over $675,000 and couples with estates over $1.35 million. Even if you have a living trust, you will pay estate taxes unless you take steps to avoid them.

- **Long Term Care protection or qualification for Medicaid** – We act as brokers (not salespeople) to find you the best coverage within your budget for long term care protection. Call for our article "Six Ways to Reduce Long Term Care Insurance Costs."

- **Investment Management** - Our investment philosophy is designed to enhance clients' success by establishing a growing portfolio that optimizes returns and lowers volatility. Our mechanical system based upon a Nobel Prize winning strategy eliminates poor judgment and errors in reasoning.

- **Annuities and Insurance** – Get the highest returns to shelter assets and defer taxes. Call our office to learn how to pass your annuity to your heirs tax-free or learn of the highest annuity rates in the country (973) 564-6565. You won't see these rates from your broker.

- **Unique Solutions to Problems**
  - How to sell real estate or stock without capital gains.
  - How to pass assets to the next generation and beyond without estate tax.

Many seniors can better organize their affairs when they know about many solutions available beyond what they are told by their stockbrokers, financial planners and lawyers. Diversified Capital Advisors first educates seniors about their alternatives, and then assists them to implement the proper solutions. The firm holds monthly seminars in the Northern New Jersey Area. For the date of our next seminar, phone 800-664-3630.

Registered Representative offering Securities and Investment Advisory Services Through Financial Network Investment Corporation, A Registered Broker/Dealer, Registered Investment Advisor, Member SIPC. Financial Network Investment Corporation and Diversified Capital Advisors, Inc. are not affiliated FNIC Branch Office: 2 Ethel Road, Suite 201 A – Edison, NJ 08817 – Telephone – (732) 248-9400

APPENDIX

The Cost and Coverage of 10 Standard Medi-gap Policies
A Through J

Plan	Cost	Basic Benefit	Hospital Deductible	Skilled Nursing Home Co-Pay	Deductible for Doctor	Foreign Travel	At Home Recovery	Excess Doctor Charges	Preventative Screening	Outpatient Prescription Drugs
A	$476	x								
B	$668	x	x							
C	$804	x	x	x						
D	$734	x	x	x	x	x	x			
E	$751	x	x	x		x				
F	$1,012	x	x	x	x	x		100%	x	
G	$896	x	x	x		x	x	80%		
H	$1,153	x	x	x		x				basic
I	$1,480	x	x	x		x	x	100%		basic
J	$1,887	x	x	x	x	x	x	100%	x	extended

82